THREE WAYS HOME

A DRAMA IN TWO ACTS

By
CASEY KURTTI

SAMUEL FRENCH, INC.
45 West 25th Street   NEW YORK 10010
7623 Sunset Boulevard HOLLYWOOD 90046
LONDON   TORONTO

Copyright © 1988, 1989 by Casey Kurtti

ALL RIGHTS RESERVED

CAUTION: Professionals and amateurs are hereby warned that THREE WAYS HOME is subject to a royalty. It is fully protected under the copyright laws of the United States of America, the British Commonwealth, including Canada, and all other countries of the Copyright Union. All rights, including professional, amateur, motion pictures, recitation, lecturing, public reading, radio broadcasting, television, and the rights of translation into foreign languages are strictly reserved. In its present form the play is dedicated to the reading public only.

The amateur live stage performance rights to THREE WAYS HOME are controlled exclusively by Samuel French, Inc., and royalty arrangements and licenses must be secured well in advance of presentation. PLEASE NOTE that amateur royalty fees are set upon application in accordance with your producing circumstances. When applying for a royalty quotation and license please give us the number of performances intended, dates of production, your seating capacity and admission fee. Royalties are payable one week before the opening performance of the play to Samuel French, Inc., at 45 W. 25th Street, New York, NY 10010; or at 7623 Sunset Blvd., Hollywood, CA 90046, or to Samuel French (Canada), Ltd., 80 Richmond Street East, Toronto, Ontario, Canada M5C 1P1.

Royalty of the required amount must be paid whether the play is presented for charity or gain and whether or not admission is charged.

Stock royalty quoted on application to Samuel French, Inc.

For all other rights than those stipulated above, apply to Ellen Hyman, 422 E. 81 Street, #4C, New York, NY 10028.

Particular emphasis is laid on the question of amateur or professional readings, permission and terms for which must be secured in writing from Samuel French, Inc.

Copying from this book in whole or in part is strictly forbidden by law, and the right of performance is not transferable.

Whenever the play is produced the following notice must appear on all programs, printing and advertising for the play: "Produced by special arrangement with Samuel French, Inc."

Due authorship credit must be given on all programs, printing and advertising for the play.

ISBN 0 573 69082 0   Printed in U.S.A.

No one shall commit or authorize any act or omission by which the copyright of, or the right to copyright, this play may be impaired.

No one shall make any changes in this play for the purpose of production.

Publication of this play does not imply availability for performance. Both amateurs and professionals considering a production are *strongly* advised in their own interests to apply to Samuel French, Inc., for written permission before starting rehearsals, advertising, or booking a theatre.

No part of this book may be reproduced, stored in a retrieval system, or transmitted in any form, by any means, now known or yet to be invented, including mechanical, electronic, photocopying, recording, videotaping, or otherwise, without the prior written permission of the publisher.

IMPORTANT BILLING AND CREDIT REQUIREMENTS

All producers of THREE WAYS HOME *must* give credit to the Author of the Play in all programs distributed in connection with performances of the Play and in all instances in which the title of the Play appears for purposes of advertising, publicizing or otherwise exploiting the Play and/or a production. The name of the Author *must* also appear on a separate line, in which no other name appears, immediately following the title, and *must* appear in size of type not less than fifty percent the size of the title type.

ASTOR PLACE THEATRE

MARLYN TSAI and JOHN BARD MANULIS

in association with

NEW WRITERS AT THE WESTSIDE

present

MARY McDONNELL **S. EPATHA MERKERSON** **MALCOLM-JAMAL WARNER**

in

THREE WAYS HOME

by

CASEY KURTTI

Setting by
DONALD EASTMAN

Lighting by
ANNE MILITELLO

Costumes by
APRIL CURTIS

Sound by
DANIEL MOSES SCHREIER

Production Stage Manager
PETER C. COOK

Associate Producer
RAYMOND L. GASPARD

Executive Producer
MARC ROUTH

Directed by
CHRIS SILVA

Opening night. May 11, 1988

CAST

Sharon .... MARY McDONNELL
Dawn.................. S. EPATHA MERKERSON
Frankie.............. MALCOLM-JAMAL WARNER

PLACE

New York City

TIME

Present

THERE WILL BE ONE FIFTEEN-MINUTE INTERMISSION

Three Ways Home was originally commissioned and developed by New Writers at the Westside in 1986. The play received its first workshop in August of that year at the Bay Area Playwrights Festival in Mill Valley, California. In November, New Writers then workshopped the play, and the playwright received a grant from the Arthur Foundation to continue work on the play. In the spring of 1987 the play was given a workshop production at the Perry Street Theatre by New York Theatre Workshop and was then further developed at the Pioneer Square Theatre in Seattle Washington. The McCarter Theatre in Princeton, New Jersey, presented the first full production of the play via its New Works Project in January, 1988.

This play is dedicated to S.A.

The play was subsequently produced by the Los Angeles Theatre Center in February of 1989. It was directed by Chris Silva with the following cast:

Sharon .... DEIRDRE O'CONNELL
Dawn .... VONETTA McGEE
Frankie...................... GLENN PLUMMER

PRODUCTION NOTES

We have had the opportunity to develop *Three Ways Home* across the country with the help of enthusiastic audiences and talented actors and designers. Based on our experience both regionally and Off Broadway we are convinced that the production (music, performance, lights, etc.) be relentless.

Instead of shying away from the "in your face" style (to say nothing of those epic opening monologues) it should be embraced. Stopping to indulge a "feeling," "explain" oneself, play a "moment," etc. is dead wrong and should be avoided at all cost. Instead the actors should try to understand and passionately embrace their characters' burning desire to tell this story and to be heard.

Part of the impulse to write *Three Ways Home* was my desire to tell the inner story of some seemingly familiar people. We think we know these people as soon as they appear on stage and yet we find out we don't. It is essential that the actors deal with the material honestly and directly, avoiding cliches of behavior. For example, Frankie should be played primarily as an uncomfortable adolescent kid, not as some psycho ready to come apart at the seams. As for Dawn and Sharon, they are parallel characters from two very different worlds, yet they both share a rich cynicism and sense of humor. They are both "tough bitches." Dawn should not be played as some bitter, down-trodden welfare mother in second-hand clothing. Nor should Sharon be played as some neurotic pin-striped Yuppie victim. They are far more complicated and evolved than those stereotypes.

The play is written and is to be performed in a presentational manner. The characters only speak to each other where indicated. So the actors will spend a majority of their time directly engaged with the audience, the "Fourth character" (who we've found occasionally takes on a life of its own). Don't try to manipulate them, just tell the story.

And one truly final thought: If you can't do the language, don't do the play.

       Casey Kurtti
       Chris Silva

       New York City, July 1988

CHARACTERS

SHARON CONWAY, 32

DAWN TOWERS, 30

FRANKIE TOWERS, 16

TIME

The Present

PLACE

New York City

THREE WAYS HOME

ACT I

SCENE: An open area surrounded on the perimeter by fire escapes, a rooftop. The feeling is tall, urban, cool. An old couch indicates Dawn's apartment. A wicker chair indicates Sharon's apartment. Down left wall a pay phone, down right wall a wireless phone.

AT RISE: RAP MUSIC is heard while HOUSE LIGHTS remain up. The MUSIC gradually begins to get louder and louder. HOUSE LIGHTS dim as FRANKIE appears from the back of the audience. He dances down the aisle, jumps on stage as the music shifts, and an incredible LIGHT SHOW begins as he continues dancing. SHARON appears upstage right and walks center stage. FRANKIE dances in front of her, then moves away. He points to her, snaps his fingers. The MUSIC stops, LIGHTS change. FRANKIE Exits and SHARON begins speaking.

SHARON. Okay, okay, let's start at the beginning. One day I'm riding the subway, trying to avoid looking at the guy with no legs. He doesn't even have a waist. He's tied to a skateboard, moving thru the car, panhandling. The first time I saw him I was so moved I gave him five dollars, but now I can't bear the sight of him. So I look at the ads above me. Next to this Puerto Rican Rum ad is one of those public service announcements. It's a photograph of a small child. He had been beaten up, had a black eye and looked incredibly sad. The copy above his picture said, "WOULD YOU LIKE TO MEET THE PERSON WHO DID THIS?" *(pause)* The panhandler was dangerously close to my ankles so I reached up and tore off one of the mailing cards and tossed it into my pocketbook. A few days later I saw it on the bottom of my bag. The kid's face was getting further abused from my make-up so in a semi-vulnerable, quasi-humanitarian moment I filled out the card and sent it in. I forgot about it until their office called me a month later. They wanted to screen me as a potential volunteer. Shit! ... Well occasionally acceptance throws me way off course so I agree to go on a face-to-face interview. The senior staff member, Janet Churchill, greets me with a big hug and as I squeeze into a nursery school chair she starts asking me very personal questions. As I talk about my own alleged childhood I just kind of stare at the artwork on the wall. On the door is one of those "HANG IN THERE, BABY" posters. You know the one with the cat hanging from the rope? I hate that poster and I take it as a sign that I should not volunteer for this program ... I immediately confess that my grandmother was insane, that my mother was emotionally unavailable, that I've been in therapy twice a week for the last five years and to top it all off, I've had severe excema my entire life. But the interviewer smiles. She says my 'honesty and vulnerability' impress her? She says I can start the training next month. Huh? SHE'S NUTS! Are they so desperate that they'll take anybody and stick them on the front line? Believe it or not I actually show up for the first training session. My benign belief in destiny frequently leads me down the wrong path. Anyway, I hide behind the September issue of Spy Magazine as the parade of neo-yuppies, housewifes and ex-candy strippers skip into the room. After a rambling welcoming speech, Janet the social worker tells us that the first thing we will do is go around the room and state what brought us here. I hate that kind of thing. Going around the room. I slump down on my folding chair and begin to make up little stories about them instead of listening to their responses so I'm a little startled when it's my turn; "Hi, I'm Sharon Conway..." Ah, I freeze. I don't have a reason to explain why I'm here. I'm not going to tell these strangers I was ignoring a cripple on the subway, so I pull it together and say, "To tell you the truth, I'm not usually drawn to acts of salvation. Hey I don't even have a savings account." I smile but no one responds. "To tell the truth I don't know what I'm doing here, except that kid's face did get to me." Well after I've "shared" we get down to business. We have only six weeks to learn the ins and outs of child abuse, the welfare system and non-judgemental behavior. We begin this crash course with a film strip on the characteristics of an abused child and abusive parent. After the lights come on I notice that some of the volunteers are crying. I mean did I miss something? The social worker asks for "feelings?" I feel nothing. But I lie and say "I feel more informed." In general, I hate quitting things in the middle, so I figure I'll just coast through the whole training and drop out at the end. Hopefully by that time they'll have figured out I don't have the right attitude.

Anyway, the third week of training we start by going around the room and "sharing" what we don't like about ourselves. I could say my overwhelming pessimism about the future of the human race, but I say my hair. Because it's no one's business. This program isn't about changing my life, it's about changing someone else's life. I miss the fourth week of the training because I was in an extremely bitchy mood. See I had just returned from a horrific weekend with my asshole boyfriend. It looked like we were heading for a definite date with a dumpster. My life as I knew it was ending. GOD I HATE CHANGE! To cushion the blow, I took a five hour bath and started reading that new Thomas Merton biography. You know "A Saint is the Act of Being Yourself"? It didn't help. I hate myself. So I'll never be a saint, who cares. I drag myself to the last week of the training. We have to go thru this psycho drama thing. I can tell that some of these people can't wait to get a hold of my jugular. Especially this woman from Queens. She tells me that I'm a CYNICAL JUDGEMENTAL HOT SHOT!!! That I may turn off an abusive mother because of my ego. EGO!!! I feel like slapping her face, but we're not allowed to respond. Thank God the meeting ends. We have to wait around because they're going to tell us whether we're accepted or not. I go hide in the bathroom upstairs and smoke twelve cigarettes in a row. I'm a wreck. And I don't know if it's because I want to kill that woman from Queens or because I'm actually starting to care about being accepted into this program. This may be my last opportunity to actually give my life a purpose, and I'm not going to let that jerk take it away from me. After an hour in the bathroom they call me into the office. I immediately start to defend myself. Apologizing for not spreading my human fraility cards out on the damn table. But they interrupt me and start listing my assets. I have the ability to show someone that with honesty and a sense of humor life can be changed. Big deal. They're just softening the blow. I'm getting ready to leave but they hand me this piece of paper to sign and say "Congratulations! You've been accepted." I leave that office floating on air. Feeling great about spending a year of my life with a woman who abuses her kids.

(LIGHTS out on SHARON. FRANKIE reappears on the fire escape. Loud RAP MUSIC begins. DAWN Enters and walks center stage. FRANKIE points to her, snaps his fingers. The MUSIC stops, LIGHTS change. FRANKIE Exits and DAWN begins speaking.)

DAWN. I don't like other people putting their face into my business. There's always some agency on my ass. Spying, taking notes ... I stay to myself. It's me and my kids. Period. You let the wrong person in you don't know what the fuck could happen. See, I'm in shit now because of my old man, James. He used to go with this crazy Puerto Rican bitch from the Bronx. She's found the number of the Bureau of Child Welfare and now my ass is grass. She tells a BCW worker that it's "Her duty to inform..." that I'm upstairs night after night beating the shit out of my four kids. The truth of the matter is that she pissed 'cause I'm living with her ex-old man. Them Puerto Rican chicks go crazy if you mess with their men. They'll come after you with a knife, throw acid in your face. Believe it. But this bitch is sneaky. She not going to go face to face with me. She knows I'll kick her ass. Word! So she drops a dime and now I got to drag my ass to Family Court. So, hey, Miss Puerto Rico gets her way this time. The fat-ass judge sentences me to this program — tells me this therapy's going to make me a better mother. He's giving me an opportunity, do I want to take it? So now I got to tell my life story to some worker once a week for God knows how long or he's going to take away my kids ... And no one is going to take away my kids. Check it out. The worker they assign me to is this skinny-ass white bitch, Janet Churchill. The first thing she says is "Why don't you tell me a little bit about yourself?" I hate that fucking question. And besides, which little bit did she want to know? I told her to call my worker at Welfare and get a blow-by-blow account. She says, "I think you're feeling a little anger about being here?" Wow! What a brain-iac! I mean this THERAPIST got all that paper, diplomas and whatnot and she doesn't know how to talk to me. White people are whack! So she keeps talking her line. Looking at my file, keeping up with her Miss Nice Personality. All chit chat. Then she gets into my face, goes deep into my business and says, "When was the first time you noticed your father had a penis?" As far as I'm concerned that came out of nowhere. I said, "Look, bitch, I didn't look down there. Ever. You want to know what I remember about my father's body? The back of his neck, his shoulders. The suitcase he was carrying. That's all I remember. Him walking out the damn door." PENIS!

JESUS CHRIST! So I don't show up for the second appointment. I'm afraid I'll punch the shit out of that worker. I've got to give myself the opportunity to chill. You dig? Anyway, when I do show up the next time, Ms. Whack Worker don't say shit about me missing the session. She all cooled out, must have got her some last night. Hair down on her shoulders. Not in that stupid ponytail. I tell her "I like your hair like that." She says, "You do? I usually don't wear it like this because it's such a bother." A bother? Right. Everything's so complicated with white people. It's all such a big deal. I tell her "You should try living my life for a day or two if you really want to see what being bothered is all about." Then I'm in for it, because that let's her jump right in there with her psycho shit. "Really, Dawn, why don't you tell me what your day is like? Why don't you start with this morning?" I tell her "Look, I gotta live it. That's bad enough. I'd kill myself if I had to run through it again on video tape for you." So the next couple of weeks was okay. Status quo. But then my oldest, Frankie had to fuck everything up. See, I had to take my youngest, James Junior, to the hospital over the weekend beause he fell out of bed. THAT'S FACT. I was out getting milk, Frankie was supposed to be in charge, watching the kids. But he left his twelve year old sister Tawny in charge and went up on the roof to read comics. All of a sudden he thinks he's King Fucking Tut. He's got a whole life going for himself up on that roof. He stores his stuff up there. Hey, I ain't insulted. I don't have enough room for all his shit down here. He's got a stack of comic books five feet high. That's just for starters. Ever since he turned 16, he's been acting whack.

Slipping in school, disrespecting me and what not. And lately he comes home with all kinds of things ... tapes, Sony Walkmen. Says his friends gave it to him ... Yeah right. I tell him "If I catch you messing with them crack heads I will kill you." Anyway, check it out, I'm gone 20 minutes, 10 minutes to the A and P, 10 minutes back. I walk into that apartment and there's my baby on Tawny's lap screaming. Blood dripping down his little face. Oh, I broke. I wrapped the baby in his little blanket and I ran over to St. Luke's Hospital. They keep me waiting four fucking hours in that emergency room. Haitain nurses be scoping me, giggling. I feel like I got a big arrow pointing over my head saying, "YOU FUCKED UP." Finally the doctor gets his shit together. He takes one look at James Junior and says "You're an abusive mother, you know that?" I explain that the baby has fallen out of bed. He says "Yeah, sure." But he lets me take my baby. As soon as I sign some papers, I'm on the bus uptown to see Janet. I get there I tell her my side of the story and she believes me! Tells me that she'll stand by me if the hospital tries to mess with me. So I get ready to leave but she says, "It must have been painful to be treated like that." "Hey that's the story of my life. But I get over." She says, "Who else treated you like that?" "Well my mother used to tell me that I was found under a garbage can. That I wasn't born in a hospital. When she was angry, which was all the damn time. She'd say 'Born the same way. Die the same way.' You see I may not have too many 'feelings' but one thing I do know, I ain't garbage." Janet gets up and puts her arms around me and you know what? She starts CRYING. I tell you this bitch is whack! ... After she blows her nose, she says, "Perhaps you'd like some more support in your life." She wants to assign me a volunteer. Some do-gooder who'll hang around with me, like a best friend. I tell her I got enough agencies involved in my business as is. And anyway I can't deal with another white bitch. But Janet reminds me that she's saving my ass with the hospital so could I "Check it out for a month?" All right, send the bitch over...

(Loud RAP MUSIC begins as FRANKIE Enters. He "sneaks" downstage center. MUSIC ends. Silence. He removes sunglasses and speaks.)

FRANKIE. Yo, what's up? My Mom's got all these people now, first James, then her psycho worker, now this new other one. Soon you're going to see the whole Secret Service pull up here and act as her damn body guard. I mean WORD, she's got all these people around her so now I got to climb in the back seat? I used to be Numero Uno around here till James came on the scene. Dude shows up smack dab on my thirteenth birthday. Ruins my whole life. 'Cause he got between me and my Moms. We used to be like this. But he messed up something that can't be put back together. Now I'm just supposed to hang around and do household chores? Yo, do I look like Mary Poppins to you? I got things to do, so let James watch the kids. I hate that guy. He doesn't do anything anyway. Just leans on my ass. It's not like he's my damn father! It's because of him I can't stand it around here, so I'm changing things around... *(Pulls out an X-Men comic book.)* ... See I'm modeling myself after the X-

Men. You ever hear of them? I'll tell you a little bit about them. My older brothers and a couple of sisters started making their appearance around 1967 in a comic book about their lives. They're stationed on this here planet. Sometimes they travel to other worlds, secret locations. they're all mutants ... Fucked up. Bent out of shape. But they're not just fucked up. They got some kick-ass powers. That's why after some serious research I hooked up with the X-Men. See, you got some sleeping creatures hiding in these here buildings. *(Leaps onto fire escapes.)* One time, three years ago, they tried to grab a hold of my sister Tawny. I saved her but they got a hold of my ass. They messed me up — tried to do me like a girl — so my Moms took me to this place where they ask you a lot of questions you don't want to explain. I went back twice. Then I cured myself. Started reading The X-Men and I learned how to get my guard up. *(Begins "acting out" Wolverine fantasy.)* See this here world fears them because they're different. I dig them cause they're not all good or bad. That's the way I am. Not all good or all bad. You dig? Well take Wolverine ... Man ... He's a hairy ass Mother Fucker with razor sharp claws. They're made of adamantium, that's the strongest metal known to mankind. Wolverine is all messed up in the face, but basically a very nice person. Sometimes I go over to Central Park and listen to my sounds. Think about them coming to life, making an appearance. To teach me about the powers. So I can prepare for my life, take care of James and some other things. They could show up one of these days. It's possible. Then I won't have to be alone. Learning all about life by myself. But I'm doing okay. Right now I'm teaching myself how to disappear. Check it out.

(FRANKIE gestures and disappears, LIGHTS up on SHARON.)

SHARON. Maybe I was getting into a little bit more than I could handle. Raped at 13!! MY GOD!!! I told Janet, wait a minute, I'm a computer animator. I don't have any psychological training. Maybe I could be reassigned to someone else? Janet smiled and said I was a perfect positive match for Dawn. Me positive? Come on! She put her hand around my shoulder and said "Trust me." Then she started endlessly listing my character atributes so I said "Okay, okay." Dawn didn't have a phone so I had to write her a note to make the first contact. I stopped at that big Hallmark place on Fifth Ave. to find the right card. I wrote "Dear Dawn. Looking forward to meeting you and your four kids. I've got lots of great plans for us. Heard you're a real wonderful person." Then I hesitated. Do I sign "LOVE" or not? I mean I did love her already. The way you love humanity generally but not specifically. I wasn't going to sign "Yours Truly" or "Sincerely." I solved it by signing it "L-U-V, Sharon." That was the way we signed our cards in high school so no one would think you were a lesbian.

(LIGHTS out on SHARON, up on DAWN.)

DAWN. "LUV." L-u-v, Sharon? What is she, one of them British bitches or something? Hey I don't want no foreigner in my life. You spell love, L-O-V-E. Damn.

Frankie brought the card over to Bellevue Hospital. I wasn't there cause I bugged out! I had female trouble. I didn't call her right away. I waited a few days. Then I said to myself, oh, let me get this shit over with fast. *(Picks up phone receiver.)* "Hi. This is Dawn."

(LIGHTS up as SHARON picks up phone receiver.)

SHARON. "Dawn who?"
DAWN. "DAWN TOWERS! That's who!"
SHARON. To tell the truth, I was a little hung over, so at first I didn't know who it was. "Oh, Dawn. Right. I'm sorry. I'm glad you called me."
DAWN. "Oh you're glad? So glad you didn't even know who I was. Shit. I heard you went through some kind of training and you don't even know what my name is?"
SHARON. WHOA! I've got two choices here: I can overcompensate or lie. "Dawn, I'm sorry. I was taking a nap, you woke me out of a sound sleep."
DAWN. "Well excuse me, Mrs. Donald Trump. Perhaps I should call you back later?"
SHARON. "No. No. Dawn, I'm glad you called. I've been dying to talk to you..."
DAWN. "Oh you've been dying to talk to me? All of a sudden there's a shortage of your own kind out there?"
SHARON. Jesus. I've got one defensive Black woman here. I'm supposed to be perfect. Not make one mistake or I go straight to Honkie Hell.
DAWN. "Look I don't know shit about you but I know you know all about my stuff."

SHARON. "Janet did give me a brief..."

DAWN. "I can hear you white girls now. Dawn was kicked out of her apartment at twelve, had her first kid, Frankie, at fourteen. Then she got herself a husband and had twins. Dumped him. Now she's got a new man, James. She got four kids now. Been on welfare for sixteen years. You know, the same old story, sits in her house watching soap operas, beating her kids and eating barbeque potato chips."

SHARON. "Actually she left out the part about the potato chips..."

DAWN. "Listen Sharon, I can't stay on this phone very long. I'm not feeling up to par. I'm calling you from Bellevue. I didn't bug out. I had female trouble. And I got to rest here a few days. I had a cyst or some shit removed from my ovary."

SHARON. "Ovary? Are you in a lot of pain?"

DAWN. "Cool out girl. I still got another one. And I'm going put that on double overtime." *(DAWN laughs to herself.)*

SHARON. "Dawn, you know you have a really nice voice. You really do..."

DAWN. "You think so? This is the voice I use when I have to talk to white people. Ain't that whack?"

SHARON. "Yeah it's whack. Real whack." Godammit! This woman is a class A bitch. Non-judgemental behavior, give me a break. Hopefully before I meet her I will have cooled down enough so I won't put her head thru a wall.

(LIGHTS out on SHARON.)

DAWN. Well I turned that Miss Goody Two Shoes upside down. She's got herself a little temper. This is going to be fun. I invite her over to my place. Let her see the whole thing from jump.

(LIGHTS out on DAWN. FRANKIE appears on fire escape.)

FRANKIE. She comes home from the hospital all high and mighty. She doesn't even thank me for keeping the place up. Doesn't notice that I painted the living room while she was gone! Fixed the twins bunk bed. X-cetera, X-cetera. Doesn't give me no credit, she just bitches about me eating some LeMenus out the freezer. I tell her things been in there so long they got freezer burn. She's just pissed because James didn't come see her in the hospital. My man used that opportunity to go on a full scale pussy patrol. And now he's A.W.O.L., so she takes it out on me. I tell her to get off my ass. Tell her to take it to her psycho worker. She tries to apologize but I'm out the door heading for the roof to chill. I'm only up there a few minutes and I hear this loud crash. Shit! MY MOMS!

(FRANKIE races down fire escape into DAWN'S space.)

DAWN. Night before Ms. Sharon's supposed to come over and run a white glove over this place, the ceiling falls down. Plaster all over. Had to clean it up by myself. You know who was on the night shift. Frankie came down from the roof. Kid was freaked, hands shaking, practically got tears in his eyes. Thought I got hurt or some shit. I tell him "Hey, I'm indestructible, but you ain't.

Not yet. So watch it." Took him awhile to chill, things always affect him too much. That's his Number One problem. I put him to work, helping me clean up ... Just me and him talking laughing almost like when he was little ... *(FRANKIE hides behind couch, jumps up, scares DAWN. They laugh together.)*

DAWN. Then we moved into his bedroom and I found one of those little Watchmen's, that little TV, stuffed under his bed. He tells me.

FRANKIE. "Mom, I didn't steal it!"

DAWN. "Then where the hell did you get it?"

FRANKIE. "A friend of mine gave it to me."

DAWN. "I hate a kid who steals and then lies about it." Get out of my house." *(FRANKIE stomps off.)* Took me five and half hours to clean up. I took a shower then I waited for Sharon out on my fire escape. My buzzer don't work and I don't want her screaming up here. The whole building knows my business as is. I know she's going to be on time. She seems like the type. At exactly eleven o'clock I see her walking down the street looking around like she don't know where she's going. Dressed in some funny-ass clothes. Shit! I got a skinny-ass white girl who ain't never seen Manhattan Avenue.

(LIGHTS up on SHARON with a bouquet of roses.)

SHARON. I had gotten up at five thirty that morning to figure out what to wear. I didn't want to give Dawn any additional ammunition for character target practice. In the training they told us to bring a tangible gift. And even though they had "This is our first date, please like me" written all over them, I settled on flowers. They're safe on all occasions? Right? When I got to her block I could see her hanging from the window. At least I thought that was her.

DAWN. I hit her on the head with my keys. By mistake. She comes up the stairs like she needs an oxygen tank. I open the door and she's got this great big fucking smile on her face and she hands me a bunch of roses. Shit. "Flowers? Hey, I ain't dead yet!" *(SHARON does a take.)* "You give flowers to dead people. Throw them on the grave."

SHARON. "Dawn there are other occasions to give flowers. Mother's day, ... Valentine's Day."

DAWN. "Hey, a chick don't give another chick flowers. Now sometimes a dude might give a bitch flowers."

SHARON. "I brought these flowers as a sign of friendship. I give flowers to my friends. Now if you don't want them..."

DAWN. "Nahhh. I'll take the shit. I just ain't used to getting flowers off a chick." She looks kind of flushed from the stairs and all. She's just standing there, getting on my last nerve. "Sharon why don't you sit down or something? *(SHARON sits on DAWN'S couch, waves dust from her face.)* You got some British background, don't you?"

SHARON. "Actually I'm not British. My great grandmother was from Ireland though. *(pause)* It's real close to England."

DAWN. "Girl, believe it or not I've seen the way this here planet is laid out. Do I look that ignorant to you?"

SHARON. "No, Dawn. I was just making a stab at conversation."

DAWN. "Well, hey, let me take charge of that. Cause you just gonna fuck it up. Now that card you sent me? You signed it LUV. L-U-V. That's why I thought you were British okay?"

SHARON. "Yeah okay." *(pause)* We just sit there in silence for awhile. She wants to call the shots, fine. I just stare at the fly strip hanging from the ceiling. I'm counting all the little dead fly bodies. I get up to 167 corpses and finally she says...

DAWN. "You want to see the place? Since you dragged your ass all the way over here. I'll give you a tour ... *(DAWN rises. SHARON follows.)*

SHARON. "Great ... Dawn, you've got fascinating, I mean beautiful hair. Is it all yours?"

DAWN. "Is it on my head?"

SHARON. "Ahh, yeah, but..."

DAWN. "But what? Tina and Cheryl upstairs in 5F hook me up. I don't go to no salon. This head's on layaway. Put that in your spy report."

SHARON. SPY REPORT? God, I didn't think she had noticed I had been casing the place. So far her place looked fine. She even had the kid's Halloween drawings taped on the cracked plaster. Maybe she just decorated for my benefit? Dawn heads towards the bedroom and I try to dust off the bottom of my pants without being too obvious.

DAWN. "This is a railroad apartment. It's got three tiny rooms. But I work with what I got."

SHARON. "Yeah I can see that. And it must be hard to

keep up with four kids..."

DAWN. "You like animals Sharon?"

SHARON. "Yeah." Good thing because she's got two large dogs, a German Shepherd and some unidentifiable canine.

DAWN. "Now I got these suckers for protection. They stay right on it. I don't have no problems with them, ever. That couch you sat on is where I sleep with my old man. I put that curtain up but the kids tear it down. They try to scope James and me at night when we're trying to do our business."

SHARON. "Dawn, I'm really glad you invited me to your place..."

DAWN. "Hey don't get so cocky. I invited you here to check you out. I don't want to embarrass myself with some white bitch Goody Two Shoes on the street."

SHARON. White bitch I can understand. BUT GOODY TWO SHOES?

DAWN. "Now that you seen the place what do you want to do?"

SHARON. "Well, we could go have lunch."

DAWN. "Lunch. Right. Tea time. I'll get the baby ready in his little Nikes and we'll go have tea and crumpets with the Queen."

SHARON. "Dawn, look we can skip lunch if you've got other plans for the afternoon..."

DAWN. "Well, I got to hook up with Cher at Jack LaLanne's and pump some iron. But I guess I can squeeze lunch in. As long as it's fast."

(LIGHT shift to indicate new space.)

SHARON. Fast. Great. Now we were talking the same language. It was suggested in the training that we take our mothers for a meal to someplace familiar to them. Like Burger King or McDonald's. So that's where we went. We got Whoppers, french fries, shakes and a burger for the baby.

DAWN. "And get get me one of them little paper crown hats for James Junior."

SHARON. It came to fifteen dollars. "Fuck this! Next time we'll go to a place I know."

DAWN. She bugged out when she saw the bill. I had to laugh when she said "Fuck this." White people are so funny when they try to get tough.

SHARON. She put the paper crown hat on James Junior, wrapped up the burger and said,

DAWN. "Yo, Sharon don't call me, I'll call you." *(DAWN Exits.)*

SHARON. I have to admit. I was glad to see her go. As I sat paralyzed, stuffing my face with the remainder of Dawn's cold french fries, this wave of unexplained "feeling" hung over my head (like a greasy halo). What in the hell was going on? I had to take three trains to get here. Some little kid spit on me on the way up her stairs. I could get shot up here and no one would ever find me. Was my desire to give my life a purpose and in turn rack up Judeo-Christian Brownie points so desperate that I could put up with Dawn's bullshit? The bus boy was giving me weird looks so I threw away my paper crown hat and went home. I waited a few days, then I called Janet and gave her my spy report, editing out the parts that made me look like a total asshole. Janet said that Dawn's reaction was to be expected. She suggested that I wait until Dawn decided to get in touch. A month and a half passed and just as I was getting very optimistic about Dawn being permanently out of my life, the phone rings...

(LIGHTS up on both women on phone.)

DAWN. "Ahh, hey, Sharon. This is Dawn. You know, Dawn Towers?"

SHARON. "I know who it is, Dawn. How could I forget you?"

DAWN. "Oh, yeah. listen I was wondering? See my check is a little late this week ... and I need Pampers for James Junior. He's been wearing the same one for five hours. Could get toxic shock or some shit. You think you could come by right now with a box?"

SHARON. RIGHT NOW??? Christ. We're moving up quickly from verbal insults to guilt tripping. "Dawn I'm really glad you called but..."

DAWN. "BUT WHAT?"

SHARON. "BUT I just can't leave work right now."

DAWN. "Yeah well I knew I shouldn't have called you ... 'BYE."

SHARON. "Dawn wait a minute..." I put her on hold to think. According to the training asking for concrete things means the client trusts you. In this case I sincerely doubt it. But hey this isn't life or death, it's a box of Pampers. "Dawn, can't you send one of the kids over?"

DAWN. "... Ah, yeah ... I'll try to get hold of Frankie."

(LIGHTS go out on DAWN.)

SHARON. "Okay, I'll be here till five." I go out on my lunch hour and buy the Pampers. Those things cost twelve dollars a box. I wait for Frankie to show up all afternoon. I can't wait to see this kid. I even practice the appropriate psychological questions to ask him. But by 6:00 I figure he's not coming. Christ. I'm disappointed and disgusted. And I'm stuck with these diapers under my desk. I head toward the door and guess who makes an appearance...

(FRANKIE Enters. His back is towards the audience.)

SHARON. Tells me they stopped him downstairs. Almost wouldn't let him in. I hate to say it but I can see why... 'Cause he's dressed in this—*(FRANKIE turns around.)*

SHARON. Ninja outfit. Sans sword, thank God. *(FRANKIE stands at attention.)* "Frankie? Hi. I'm Sharon. I have the Pampers for your Mom." *(FRANKIE moves around stage Ninja style.)* "So ... ummm. That's a nice mask you have on. Where did you get it?" *(FRANKIE ignores her.)* "Well umm. You want to walk downstairs together?" *(FRANKIE shakes head.)* "Frankie, what's with you? You need a token? I'm not going to play 20 questions with you."

FRANKIE. "What kind of computer is that?"

SHARON. "Oh. It's an Edge Vanguard Mini-Super Computer, top of the line. Isn't it cool? Hey, would you like to see a video of mine? Check out what I do?" *(FRANKIE shrugs his shoulders. SHARON pulls a remote control from her pocket.)* "This demo is sort of lame. It's a dancing pineapple commercial. But the music is good."

(SHARON presses button. LIGHTS change. FRANKIE removes his mask.)

FRANKIE. "Snap! How do you keep changing the picture into something else?"

SHARON. "That's interpolation. Just one of those magical things we do in computer graphics..."

FRANKIE. "I ain't no third grader. Explain it to me."

SHARON. "Okay. You bring me a two dimensional object. Your company's logo for example. And I put in on my digitalizing tablet. Tracing the outline with a cursor..."

FRANKIE. "It goes into the computer and it turns into three dimension?"

SHARON. "Exactly. Well you seem to have a feel for this. You want to see another one?"

FRANKIE. "No. Change me."

SHARON. "What?"

FRANKIE. "Change me into this." *(Pulls out X-Men. SHARON looks.)*

SHARON. "This guy? With the cigar?"

FRANKIE. "Yeah, Wolverine."

SHARON. "Wolverine? Never heard of him. Richie Rich, Archie, G.I. Joe..."

FRANKIE. "G.I. Joe's a pussy! Travels with weaponry. X-Men don't need no weapons. They travel with the power inside of them."

SHARON. "He's got a kimono on ... he's Japanese?"

FRANKIE. "Nobody knows where he's from, his papers say Canada, but dude's got pure samari in his heart. This is an old issue. See, he was supposed to get married to this Japanese babe Lady Mariko. The whole family was supposed to attend. But in the next issue it gets all fucked up. His heart gets broken. Being a mutant don't X-empt you from all the shit. Let's go, juice it up..."

SHARON. "This will take time. Frankie, we'll start it today and then you can come back some other time?" *(FRANKIE smiles.)* I take the comic book and start processing it. Frankie stands there laying these instructions on me every once in awhile.

FRANKIE. "Those claws ain't long enough. Got to do it over."

SHARON. It takes me two hours to come up with a final product that meets with his approval. This kid's a perfectionist. I take him up to the screening room and set it up on this big monitor, turn off all the lights and...

(LIGHTS down on SHARON. FRANKIE is suddenly covered in an eerie GREEN LIGHT. A computer like MUSICAL TONE begins to be heard and grows in volume under FRANKIE'S monologue.)

FRANKIE. Yo, check it out! This is fly. This is funky. This is the move. This is me. The Real Me. Like I was meant to be. An X-Man. Ohh you got to be-lieve!!! See I told you the X-Men were slick. I dig this computer shit. Makes you think a whole nother life is possible. Almost like Wolverine cut right into Sharon's machine and sent me this picture. Snikt, Snikt. Telling me there's a chance I'll be accepted for membership into the family. Then I'd have to go home and pack up my stuff. Kiss all the kids good-bye. Enroll in Professor X-Avier's School for Gifted Youngsters up in Westchester County. (That's where all the X-Men go to learn the mutant ways.) My Moms would have tears in her eyes seeing me fly off with my new brothers but I'd promise to come back and visit if I had a mission in the neighborhood and my schedule permitted. Then I'd make my X-it. Fire up the sky. X-ilerating! "Yo Sharon, print this shit up!"

(SOUND and LIGHTS go out on FRANKIE. LIGHTS up on DAWN.)

DAWN. Sharon sends Frankie home with the wrong size diapers. I let it slide, cause Frankie came home all fired up. In a good mood. Said Sharon turned him on to "the wonders of computer technology." Asks my permission to hang out at her office once a week and work on stuff. I tell him its cool as long as it don't involve him cutting no school or whatnot and he keeps family business out of it. Anyway, the next time I go see Janet, she gives me some line about "...not working the program..." So I call Sharon from Janet's office and ask her "Where you been? We should get together and have lunch and talk about all my problems. 'Cause Janet says we got to."

(LIGHTS shift, women meet with two chairs. They sit.)

SHARON. Dawn keeps me waiting on 57th Street for twenty minutes. I was going to give her a lecture entitled "Lateness counts" but I was so hungry, I just ended up telling her I was willing to go anywhere but Burger King."

DAWN. She takes me to Beefsteak Charlie's 'cause that's where I want to go. She orders everything diet. I order a sirloin steak, well done, french fries, and a burger for the baby. I want salad bar. But I don't want them guinea waiters scoping me. "Sharon, you gotta old man or what? What's your story?"

SHARON. "My story? ... What about you and James? How long have you been together?"

DAWN. "Girl, we discussing you. I want to get to know you better. You got an old man or what?"

SHARON. "Dawn, I'm not really sure about that. I mean it's on again, off again. Right now it's off again."

DAWN. "Yeah, well that's too bad. You gotta hook up with someone steady. Get yourself some kids. You're getting up in age. Me and James been together for three years, four months!"

SHARON. "Really? I've never been with anyone longer than two years."

DAWN. "Well girl, you go out with white boys what do you expect?"

SHARON. "Dawn!"

DAWN. "Frankie tells me that you're hooked up with computers. MTV shit. You must be pulling in some serious cash."

SHARON. "I'm doing okay."

DAWN. "Yeah, you look good today. Where'd you get that outfit?"

SHARON. "Ahh, Ann Taylor's. But I got it on sale. Over two years ago."

DAWN. "Well it's holding up nice. You got to write down the address. I'll check out Anne Taylor too."

SHARON. Jesus this is great. This is progress. Girl talk! Dawn's got to feel comfortable with me before we can move on to... *(DAWN clears her throat loudly and pulls out a Con Edison bill.)*

DAWN. "Hey, Sharon, check this out. Fucking Con

Edison sent me a shut-off notice. Electricity is off tonight."

SHARON. "Tonight?" What about all the kids sitting in the dark? The German Shepherd could get spooked and take someone's leg off. "Dawn, let's call right now and arrange a partial payment."

DAWN. "Patrial payment? Honey, we're dealing with Con Edison here. They won't accept partial payments. Not when you're four months behind. Ahhh... Sharon, I was wondering ... you're here to help me out with things, right?"

SHARON. "Right."

DAWN. "Right. Well I was wondering ... maybe you could help me out with this. Now aren't you all supposed to be helping us learn how to stretch the dollar? Makin' supper all week for $1.35 or some shit? This could be like the first lesson. See you could lend me the money for Con Ed. Then I pay you back. Say, like ten dollars a month?"

SHARON. "Ten dollars a month?"

DAWN. "Uh-huh. So Sharon what do you say? See, sister, you're the only person I can turn to."

SHARON. Did she say SISTER?

DAWN. "So can you give me the money or what?"

SHARON. "Say, Dawn, do you think I can take a look at the bill? See the way it's broken down?"

DAWN. I was glad I brought that bill with me. Proof. You know how white people are about proof. Don't nothing happen in this world without proof. "Now see here, Sharon, my bill is fifty dollars a month. That's depending on how much the kids run the TV."

SHARON. I've got to make a decision here. Do I get sucked into being CEO of Dawn's fiscal affairs or do I pass? Christ, maybe I'm making too big a deal about this. It isn't life or death, it's just an electric bill. I just have to be willing to trust that she will pay me back the...

SHARON/DAWN. "$234.56."

SHARON. "Dawn, who do I have to make the check out to..."

DAWN. "Ahh, it's got to be hand-delivered. You have to go downtown to Fourteenth Street this afternoon..."

SHARON. "I'll have to go downtown. Hey, Dawn, I got things to do..."

DAWN. "Hey, so do I. I got to go to Beth Israel for the baby's six month's shots. I'm going to be there till nine tonight. I can't squeeze Con Ed in. So I leave it up to you. We'll skip dessert. YO WAITER!!! Or do you want it to go?"

SHARON. "No, Dawn. I don't want dessert."

DAWN. "There's a Haagen Dazs right outside and we can grab a cone... Sharon, you're really helping me out. Really doing your job. You're okay for a white girl."
(DAWN Exits, SHARON stunned, holding bill.)

(BLACKOUT. FADE UP to FRANKIE sitting on the couch with a computer printout of himself as Wolverine.)

FRANKIE. See this? This used to be my computer X-Men printout. James ripped this shit right in half cause I borrowed his Fila sweatshirt without asking. Says I damaged the goods. I was so mad tears started to come to my eyes. My Moms took my side for once and chewed the mother fucker out. Then she goes to the kitchen and tries to tape the pieces back together, took her all night to straighten the shit out. When I wake up in the morning, she's got it hanging on my wall. I don't say nothing, just pretend like I'm sleeping till she leaves. *(Crumples up the printout and throws it away.)* She ain't gone but 10 minutes and you-know-who crawls out of bed, he's all smiles and whatnot. Knows he's in the D.O.G. house. But I don't say nothin'. I turn my back and split. Sign in at school and then head over to Central Park. I got to chill, you dig? I'm sitting on the grass, reading and whatnot when this dude comes up to me. He wants to know what I'm reading "X-Men, stupid." He says, "I didn't know kids still read comics." "Look man, I'm no kid. Get that straight." He gets all red in the face. He's from Jersey. Your face don't get soft like that, so fast, if you're from around here. I'm going to get over on this guy ... "Sit down. No. Over there." He does. Like a dog. He's under my command. He tells me he wants a tourguide. Tourguide my ass. I know what he wants, but I play with him. "I don't go to no museums. No cultural shit." He says "I don't like museums either. Take me to the places you want to go. Ten dollars an hour, fifty up front." I say "Seventy-five!" he bites! See I got some of the powers already. X-Men be teachin' me right!

(LIGHTS fade on FRANKIE. Stage is dark.)

DAWN. *(Flicks a butane lighter in the semi-dark.)* Now I know the girl is dizzy. You take one look at her face and you can tell that. Says she's going to do something and I take her at her mother fucking word. Big mistake. I got kids crawling all over me crying and whatnot. They can't watch TV, they're scared of the dark. What a mess.

SHIT! "DYNASTY'S" ON TONIGHT. I'm going to fry that girl. *(Crosses to phone.)* I go out on the street to call her up, got to borrow the damn money from the Vietnamese chick downstairs. Takes me a half an hour to explain what a quarter is. Anyway she ain't home. Probably out filling her face in some high class restaurant. She's got one of them damn answering machines. Some whack music playing in the background. I wait for the beep ... "Hey, Sharon, guess what, I'm sitting in the mother fucking dark. I hope they got lights on where you're at!" Then I call Janet, she's got an answering machine too. Maybe them two bitches are out together. "Hey, Janet, that white girl you assigned me to left me sitting here in the dark. I'm firing her. She don't know what she's doing. Promising me shit she can't deliver. And I don't want another one. That's it ... Oh, yeah, it's Dawn. Dawn Towers."

(LIGHTS cross fade to FRANKIE.)

FRANKIE. It's late. It's getting cold. And this dude Irwin thinks he's slick. Asks me "Have you ever been to the Waldorf Astoria?" I tell him "I've seen it from the outside." He says, "Well, why don't we go check out the inside?" We take a cab over there. I already got one hundred of his bills in my pocket and I ain't done jack. At the hotel he signs the book. And takes out a gold American Express card. "Yo, folks, do you know me? I'm Frankie X-Men Towers." Then snap. Cops are all up in our face. They take Irwin away. Leave me standing. Shit, now I'm dead. My stomach drops out. My Moms is going to kick my ass. A cop comes over to me and says, "Where do you live boy?" "103rd Street. But hey I didn't do nothing. I swear on my honor. If you don't believe me, ask Wolverine."

(LIGHTS cross fade back to DAWN.)

DAWN. I'm walking back from the phone booth and I see a police car outside my building. Frankie. How much you want to bet? Cops get all up in my face. Accuse me of sending my kid out into hotels to fuck guys to make money. I almost scratch his eyes out. Tell me they got to make a report. Did I have anything to say. "Yeah, I got something to say. I don't send my kids out into the street. They got a good home. And what about the mother fucking sleaze bag that dragged him there!!" They take my statement and Janet's phone number and they get their fat asses in their cars and take off. Frankie's got tears in his eyes. I send him upstairs and I go to call Janet on the pay phone. She's there this time. Starts in about Sharon. I tell her "Girl, that's ancient history. I got some current events for you to chew on." She goes on and on, telling me he's acting out or some shit. Telling me I should talk to him, find out what's going on in his head, let him tell me his "feelings." I tell her "Look. let me get off the phone, girl. It's freezing out here. And these cars are driving by thinking I'm selling it. "Hey stop honking that horn, I ain't no 'ho!" I went back upstairs, there's Frankie sitting in the kitchen, James Junior on his lap, the twins sitting on the floor, telling them ghost stories. He's rigged up a flashlight so it ain't pitch black. He thinks it's business as usual. I send the other kids into the bathroom to brush their teeth, so I can talk with this child in private. "Frankie, what were you doing in a hotel?"

(LIGHTS come up on FRANKIE.)

FRANKIE. "Looking at chandeliers."
DAWN. "What's goin on with you? You hurting, you come to me. I'll fix it. That's the way it's always been and that's the way it'll always be. You got a mother right here that cares about you. Okay? Okay, honey? Hey, Frankie, you listening to me? Look at me. Stand up straight and take your hands out of your pockets." *(As DAWN says the following FRANKIE performs the action.)* He looks me straight in the eye, takes his hands out his pockets and all this money hits the floor. And I'm thinking, oh, Jesus, sneakers, Sony Walkmans, cassettes, oh, Frankie...

(LIGHTS fade on DAWN.)

FRANKIE. You saw that? She cut me with her eyes. Fearing me, thinking I'm bad. What's happening with her? She's joining them out there. She's just like everybody else. I can't be down here by myself, it's too dangerous. Got to find a way to hook up with my true family. That's just the way it has to be. I can't make no more X-Ceptions. Not even for her.

(FRANKIE Exits. LIGHTS cross fade to SHARON.)

SHARON. I tried to make it down to Con Edison in time

but the God damn trains fucked me up. Couldn't get a cab so the office was closed. I slipped the check under the door and bribed the security guard to give it to someone who was working overtime. I thought about going back up to Dawn's to explain the situation. But I had had it with heroic overcompensation, so I went home. After a two hour mental gymnastic session I came to the frightening conclusion that I was basically incapable of having any sort of meaningful relationship with Dawn. Never mind transforming her life. As I was finishing my second half glass of red wine, the phone rings. It's Janet. She tells me that Frankie has just been busted for prostitution. Shit!!! Prostitution?! Janet tells me to calm down and get a good night's sleep and check in with Dawn tomorrow. A good night's sleep? Yeah, sure. This is life or death. I want to go over there right now. Janet advises me to check my answering machine before heading uptown. Dawn may need some time to cool down before she's in the mood to share her feelings with me. I rewind the tape. For once, Janet is absolutely on the money.

(LIGHT fade up on DAWN.)

DAWN. I didn't get any sleep all night. My mind kept going about Frankie. Then at 8:30 in the damn morning, Sharon is at my door with coffee and doughnuts. "Sharon, you got some fucking nerve. What are you doing here?"

SHARON. "Ahh, Dawn, I just thought that..."

DAWN. "Girl, get out the way, let me get these kids off to school and then I'll deal with you."

SHARON. I drank some coffee and tried to keep the

German Shepherd from humping my leg.

DAWN. "Tawny, feed that baby before you go. Frankie! Tabatha, pick those Cheerios up off the table. Not with your tongue."

SHARON. Finally the kids were out the door. "Dawn, I tried to get out of work on time. The damn trains were a mess. I even bribed the security guard."

DAWN. "Hey life's a bitch, ain't it? So you tried and you fucked up. So why don't you just get the hell out of here. Nothing personal, I just don't like being lied to."

SHARON. "I didn't lie to you, Dawn. I disappointed you and I'm sorry about that..."

SHARON. "...Especially after what happened last night."

DAWN. "Sorry don't cut it with me. So just hand in your walkie talkie cause I already put in for a new volunteer. You're out of the picture."

SHARON. "I'm out of the picture? I didn't deliver the goods on your schedule and now you're ready to pin my ass to the wall."

DAWN. "No, I'm just relieving you of your duties. Your fucked up ass is your business."

SHARON. "FUCKED UP ASS? This isn't about me..."

SHARON. "It's about your son."

DAWN. "Oh, yes, it is. Ain't you the fuck up that left me sitting in the dark? Speak on that!"

SHARON. "Hey you haven't paid the bill in four months. You speak on that! Now I didn't come over here to be a punching bag. I came because I was concerned about you. Janet told me that Frankie was picked up..."

DAWN. "Stay out of my business. What makes you such an expert on kids? How many you got? See, that's why I told Janet I got to replace you. You don't know shit about the things that involve me."

SHARON. "Right. I don't know shit about you."

DAWN. "Hey, you read my file. I don't have no paperwork on you! Girl, you don't know who you dealing with here. On a good day I'd kick your ass! Coming in my house, raising your voice, telling me I got to talk to you. Who the fuck are you? Some white bitch goody two shoes with some free time? Well, I don't have no free time to socialize with you. I gotta take a shower. I got to go over to P.S. 139 and pick up Tabatha's report card. So if you got anymore suggestions about how I should run my life I suggest you just write them out and send them to Janet. You're history." *(DAWN Exits.)*

SHARON. Dawn stomps into the bathroom and turns on the shower. I'm on my way out and the TV comes on. PERFECT TIMING CON EDISON!!! "HEY DAWN YOUR SERVICE HAS BEEN RESTORED! SO JUST HAVE YOUR NEW VOLUNTEER MAIL ME THE TEN DOLLARS A MONTH. AND WHILE WE'RE SETTLING ACCOUNTS LET'S GET SOMETHING STRAIGHT ONCE AND FOR ALL. I'M NO WHITE BITCH GOODY TWO SHOES. I'M A CYNICAL JUDGEMENTAL HOT SHOT WITH A BIG EGO. OH AND P.S. ON A GOOD DAY I COULD'VE KICKED YOUR ASS!!!! I don't know if she heard me ... I crawled over the German Shepherd and let myself out. I go downstairs and call Janet from the pay phone to tell her it's over. I give her a blow-by-blow account of the disaster-a-thon. When I'm finished Janet starts crying! Jesus Christ! She blows her nose and says "I'm proud of you, Sharon. You really hung in there! Dawn needs someone who will fight for her friendship. You showed her who you truely are. I wasn't sure you had it in you." WHAT!!! Then she tells me that's what the program is all about, being an honest friend. Nothing more, nothing less. I told her I had to get off the phone cause cars kept stopping and asking me how much I was selling it for. HEY, FUCK OFF!!!

(MUSIC blasts, LIGHTS fade.)

END OF ACT I

ACT II

MUSIC continues as before, loud. FRANKIE dances into LIGHT. Silence.

FRANKIE. My Moms is on a fucking rampage, thanks to Sharon and her psycho worker. Says I got to sit down with James, work out shit man-to-man. She's buggin. Tries to take me on these walks to get me to talk about my feelings. Says she wants to meet any friends I have. And that I got to start thinking about hooking up with some females. She says if I'm not with her or at school I'm supposed to stay in the house. Fuck, I feel like I'm in jail. She's always watching my ass. After a while things cool out and I hit the street. She makes me promise I won't go to Central Park, so I switch my headquarters and go downtown by the piers. *(Climbs on fire escape.)* 'Cause a man needs space and I like nature, you dig? But, hey, you gotta watch yourself down by the water cause that's where all the weirdos hang. Night before I'm supposed to go to court, I'm just sitting out there, reading and whatnot. Sun's going down. And this car pulls up. A Toyota Hatchback. I'm not getting in this shit like the last time so I say "Yo, is you a cop?" He's got to 'fess, otherwise it's entrapment. Dude says no. Tells me he'd like to take me back to his place, make me some dinner. Say's I look "hungry." Yeah right, he's the one who's licking his lips. I get in the car but first I make him stop at this video store so I can have something to watch while he's "cooking." He lets me pick the movie. I take "Poltergeist." That flick is jammin'. I've seen it twelve times. It's about this family that's haunted by ghosts that come thru a TV set. Rhino, ah ... that's the dude's name, Rhino says he's looking forward to seeing it with me. Yeah, right. We get back in the car, he touches me. I ignore him, keep talking. He starts acting a little funny. Keeps one hand on the steering wheel and pulls out this Swiss army knife with the other. Shows me this little scissor. Says he likes to get cut. Shit. He's a freak. An evil mother fucker, just like Juggernaut in issue 177 of the Uncanny X-Men. I'm in serious danger, and there's only one person who can save me. So I roll down the window and call out, WOLVERINE!!! My brother surfaces out the shadows, claws extended, jumps up on the traffic light. SNIKT, SNIKT, he turns it to red. Car stops for the light. And I jump out just as the freak goes for my throat. See, I told you, X-Men ain't no joke.

(LIGHTS fade on FRANKIE and pick up DAWN.)

DAWN. Night before we're supposed to go to Family Court Frankie fucks everything up. He keeps me waiting outside of May's for an hour. Pissed me off. I pinch pennies out of my check all month so I can come up with something respectable for him to wear to court. Don't want the kid's wardrobe to come between us, you dig? But he pulls a no-show so I got to guesstimate his size. Frankie ain't himself since the police brought him home. Won't talk to me or the kids, won't even look me in the eyes. Janet says he's in denial or some shit about what he did. Says I got to go easy on him. Yeah, right. When I get home Frankie's there all hang-dogged, apologizes for getting amnesia. I can tell he don't mean it, but I don't put him thru no 3rd degree, I just send his ass off to bed before I say something I'll regret. Next morning the damn alarm don't go off so we got to take a cab all the way downtown. That's just the beginning of the bad news 'cause guess who's assigned to the case, the same fat-ass judge that fried my ass the last time. Mother fucker stares me up and down.

(LIGHTS change to define "courtroom." FRANKIE Enters to join DAWN in "court.")

DAWN. He's one of them that never forget a face. He starts right in with some hostile legal shit telling me he's "leaning toward removing the juvenile from the home." I'm ready to go off, but Frankie squeezes my hand and Janet jumps from her chair. Goes right up to the bench and starts in with her psycho song and dance. Old Fat Ass is yawning and whatnot, he's heard it all before. So he cuts her off and asks if anybody else got something else to say.

(SHARON Enters.)

SHARON. "I do, your honor."
DAWN. Sharon? Who invited her? There's so many people by my side I feel like Chaka Fucking Khan. Judge calls her up to the bench and she puts it in overdrive. *(SHARON moves downstage to address judge.)*

SHARON. "Your honor, my name is Sharon Conway. I've been working with Ms. Towers for the past few months. In fact, you brought us together by assigning her to the program. I don't know whether to thank you or deck you one. Because frankly, Dawn Towers is far from perfect. In fact, she's a royal pain in the ass. As a client. As a mother, that's a different story. I'd classify her as exemplary. Because with little or no resources, she has attempted to make a good home for her children. On the walls of her tiny 103rd Street apartment, she has hung her children's artwork to encourage their creativity. Out of concern for their safety, she keeps two large dogs guarding the entrance to their apartment. Do you have any idea how much it costs to feed a German Shepherd? But no sacrifice is too big where her children are concerned. It is not easy for a proud woman like Dawn to ask others for help. But she called me, a relative stranger to ask for pharmaceutical supplies when her baby was in need. A few weeks later, she came to me with a plan to get her finances in order. The speed in which this woman works is blinding at times. I doubt there is another person taking so much from this program. Yet you are thinking about removing this child from his home. That doesn't make much sense to me. You've read his case file, his troubles have to do with a violation from a stranger. His mother is attempting to heal that wound with love. Don't interrupt her. The evidence is on her side. Besides, the good city of New York can't even place three-month-old babies. Where are you going to find a better home for a somewhat troubled 16-year-old? Thank you for your time, your honor, and God bless you." *(SHARON moves upstage.)*

DAWN. THE BITCH WAS FIERCE! Girl knows how to run a serious game! I'll give her that. Judge got his mouth hanging open. Then he takes a gulp, starts making a little speech about "the difficulties of proper parenting" or some shit. But he decides in my favor. Says I get to keep Frankie as long as I keep up with the program. Case dismissed. *(FRANKIE and DAWN embrace. FRANKIE high-fives SHARON and Exits.)*

SHARON. "YEAH!!!" *(DAWN and SHARON move downstage, each taking a corner.)*

DAWN. "I've decided to keep you on. Probation. So, what do you say we do something since we're stuck with each other?"

SHARON. "Dawn, why don't we got to the movies?"

DAWN. "Fine. We can go to the Deuce and see — "

SHARON. "The Deuce? Dawn, the guys are so noisy. I really hate to go to a film where the only dialogue you get to hear is the audience."

DAWN. "Hey, to me that's half the fun, the audience. You're bullshitting me. You're afraid those Puerto Ricans and 'Black People' are going to mess with your ass. You're scared but you won't admit it."

SHARON. "No I'm not! I don't want to see a shoot-um up with 4000 Uzi's. Why don't we go see a movie that's about something?"

DAWN. "Hey, I ain't going to see no Bette Midler movie, so forget it."

SHARON. "I'm not talking about Bette Midler."

DAWN. She wants to go see "The Colored People." I mean "Color Me Purple," whatever the name is.

SHARON. " 'The Color Purple.' It's playing on 8th

Street, at the revival house. I missed it the first time around."

DAWN. "Sharon, I saw the commercials for that one. And I see what you're trying to do. You're trying to take me to a movie with black folks in it."

SHARON. "No, I'm not!"

DAWN. "Look, I don't feel like arguing, we'll go see the fucking movie, alright? Cause I do owe you one."

SHARON. GLORY HALLELUIAH!!!!! *(DAWN Exits. Movie theme MUSIC begins playing softly.*)*

SHARON. Okay, okay, I admit it. I went to the movie solely for Dawn's benefit. I had no desire to see it. I had read the book and I knew Spielberg would fuck it up. He did. But I've got to admit I cried at certain points. Dawn didn't cry. She just kept jumping up, getting sodas, complaining about the popcorn. She didn't have the experience I wanted her to have. And she didn't bring her wallet. So I had just enough cash left to buy coffee for our post cinema discussion. *(DAWN Enters with two coffee cups.)*

DAWN. "I got your number girl. You think you're slick, don't you?"

SHARON. "What?"

DAWN. "You trying to draw some sort of connection between me and that Cellie bitch, right?"

SHARON. "Wrong."

DAWN. "What do you think, I'm ugly like that old Cellie?"

SHARON. "Dawn, you're beautiful. You're a pain in the

---

*Cautionary Note: Permission to produce this play does *not* include rights to use this music.

ass. But you're beautiful."

DAWN. "Well, you ain't. You got mascara all hanging down your eyes. You look like a raccoon. Why don't you wipe your eyes?"

SHARON. "Dawn, look I know the movie was whack..."

DAWN. "WHACK?"

SHARON. "Yeah, WHACK."

DAWN. "WHACK?"

SHARON. "Yeah, WHACK... I can say it too, SISTER... so chill. Now that movie still got to me. Seeing her go through all those changes."

DAWN. "Well it didn't get to me. Sitting there watching that girl get the shit beat out of her for two and a half hours by that dude from 'Lethal Weapon.' Hey, I got my own problems. Give me action adventure so I can take a break. See, that's why I wanted to go to the Deuce. You get some kick-ass laughing at that theatre."

SHARON. Ohhh, I felt like kicking her ass. I mean, I wasn't expecting her to levitate off the planet. Any crumb of emotional recognition would do. Damn it. Well, she's not budging, neither am I.

DAWN. "Now I ain't denying that there was some good parts..."

SHARON. "Really! Like what?"

DAWN. "Well Oprah tore it up."

SHARON. "You thought so? So did I."

DAWN. "No shit. When she came out of jail all fucked up I thought you was going to lose it. The way you was going on for a minute I thought maybe you had done some time ... did you?" *(SHARON crosses. Pauses.)*

SHARON. "NO!" But I almost got busted once for pot in high school."

DAWN. "Reefer? You?"

SHARON. "Yeah, Dawn! I smoked pot in high school ... and I shoplifted ... and I was expelled for sleeping with the wrestling coach. So put that in your bad-ass bong and smoke it!"

DAWN. "Bad-ass bong? Girl, you 'illin. Did you take a hit? Is that why you got into the lame-ass flick?"

SHARON. "No. Listen, Dawn, Cellie really is a great character. I really identified with her. Her courage to keep going. And I thought you would too... Maybe if you read the book. The book is so much better."

DAWN. We stop at Barnes and Nobles and she charges the fucking book.

SHARON. "Just read it. We'll get together next week and we'll discuss it. Okay?"

(SHARON Exits. LIGHTS change. DAWN sits on her couch.)

DAWN. Read a book in a week? Who did she think I was, Evelyn Wood? Girl's got problems. Later that night, after I put the kids to bed, I took a look at that book. THE COLOR PURPLE. It opens with a letter to God. I close it up right away. My thing with God ain't been too tough since I was ten. He dropped me down here and forgot about me. So I don't have nothing to do with him what-so-never. My mother is into Jesus, oh, yeah. She sends me these paint by number religious scenes every Christmas. That's the only thing she's got to say to me. She knows I won't listen to her shit. So she tries to speak another language. But them paintings don't talk to me.

God don't talk to me. I talk to myself when something needs fixing. Uh-huh. Now that stupid movie reminded me that I got some minor adjusting to do. See I still got my ex-old man's name attached to my ass and I want to cut it loose. Get on it and get a divorce. Sharon could probably hook me up with a lawyer, but I'll wait a few weeks on that. I don't want her to think that it had anything to do with that damn movie. Cause it didn't speak my language anymore than God does.

(LIGHTS cross fade to SHARON.)

SHARON. DAWN'S GETTING A DIVORCE!!!!!! We're on a roll here. The movie didn't hit her right away. I had to wait two full weeks. But finally she showed up in my office. Said she just happened to be in the neighborhood and by the way did I know anybody at Jacoby and Meyers? I immediately checked with a couple of my lawyer friends about inexpensive divorces. The cheapest they came up with was three hundred dollars. I called Legal Aid. I was on hold for twenty minutes. When they finally got around to me, they said they were too busy with criminal and civil cases. So how the hell does someone on welfare get a divorce? The lawyer told me to calm down and she gave me the number of a do-it-yourself divorce class.

(LIGHTS cross fade to DAWN.)

DAWN. There was alot of stupid-ass people in that class who dropped out. But I made it through all right. I graduated from divorce class! Luckily my ex-husband

George was cooperative. He wasn't too happy about mental cruelty and abandonment being the reason, but I told him to chill 'cause they was better than the real ones. Sharon made a big fuss when the papers came. Pats herself right on the back. Takes me out to lunch in some high class place and then drags me over to Coliseum Books. I scope the detective section but she goes over to the Woman's Book section. Buys me this book on that African chick, Winnie Mandela. I tell you that girl never gives up.

(LIGHT fades on DAWN and picks up FRANKIE, who Enters with a Casio strapped to his back.)

FRANKIE. My Moms is a divorcée now. Big fucking deal. I tell her to talk to me when she cuts James loose. Sharon got her a cake with writing on it. Said "Congratulations! On to bigger things!" We're not allowed to eat it. It's jammed in the freezer. Can't touch it till Christmas. Shit, that's three weeks away. Christmas around here always sucks. No presents, nothing. We don't even get a skinny-ass tree. Every year it gets worser. But hey, this year, I'm turning it all around. I'm in charge of Christmas. See I got myself some regular customers. I'm going full time, I'm jacking up my prices. These freaks love to party during the holidays. I'll make some serious money. Buy some nice shit. I'm going to get two Cabbage Patch Preemies for Tawny and laser tag and those fake press on nails for Tabatha. And a Big Bird chair for the baby. And I already bought myself a Deluxe Casio. So I can play some funky Christmas carols. Check it out. *(He plays "Jingle Bells" on the keyboard.)* If my Moms stays out of my face I'll get her a present, but James gets jack shit!!! I'm buying everything at F.A.O. Schwartz. That's the store where Michael Jackson had a sleep-over party. They got some fancy-ass wrapping paper over there. I go in there at least once a week to check out their inventory. Salesman be eyeballing me so much they be in pain. Waiting for me to palm a Hulk Hogan doll and stuff it down my jacket. Oh, I can't wait to make my purchases and cold laugh right in their faces. I've already got $357.00 saved up. It's right here in my sock. This is a good season for me. It's X-Mas! It's better to give than receive. Ho ho ho...

(LIGHTS cross fade back to SHARON.)

SHARON. Janet calls and tells me they're having this big Christmas party for all the abusive mothers. Santa, presents, everything. Dawn doesn't want to go. She says she doesn't want any fucked up women scoping her or her kids. Tell you the truth I don't want to go either. I don't want to see any of those volunteers, especially that woman from Queens. I tell Dawn, "Let's me and you have a private party."

(LIGHTS up on DAWN.)

DAWN. Sharon invites me to her apartment. It's about time. It's in the Village. She lives in one of them houses with nice old wood doors. Got a wreath out front. That thing wouldn't last two minutes uptown. James Junior tries to grab the little reindeer off it. But I slap his hand just in time.

SHARON. Luckily, Dawn was late. It took me a long time to get the place in order. I hid my pot, pulled any strange books off the shelf and cued up a Ricki Lee Jones record. Then I changed it to Marvin Gaye. Then I changed it to Anita Baker. I still hadn't decided on what to wear. I took off an old Laura Ashley dress cause I looked too much like Beth in "Little Women." Luckily I had wrapped Dawn's present the night before. I got her two pairs of jeans and a gift certificate to Cineplex Odeon Movie Theatres. Now I didn't want Dawn to think that I was the great big B'Wana or something, but I had tons of stuffed animals jammed into my closet and I thought she could use them for the kids. I don't know why I had been saving them. They'd been living in plastic for years.

(DAWN Enters with something hidden behind her back.)

DAWN. It takes her awhile to answer the door. I'm thinking maybe I got the wrong day or something. Shit, I even brought her a present. *(DAWN reveals a bouquet of carnations.)*

SHARON. "Dawn. Thanks. Red and green carnations. They're beautiful." *(SHARON Exits.)*

DAWN. "What's the big deal? They only cost a dollar fifty at the chink place around the corner." She looked kind of weird. Uptight or something. Probably cause she had a black velvet dress on, fancy shoes. I mean shit, it was just me and James Junior. No big deal. She even made little angel cookies, egg nog and a burger for the baby.

(SHARON Enters with two egg nog mugs.)

SHARON. I think Dawn was a little nervous about being in my house. But after a quart of egg nog we were pretty relaxed. "Bottoms up — "
SHARON/DAWN. "Again!" *(They drink and sit drunkenly on the floor.)*
DAWN. "You know I hate to say it, but this egg nog kind of reminds me of ... It's all thick and creamy..."
SHARON. "Yeah, yeah I know what you mean."
DAWN. "Check it out. Am I right? Sharon, Sharon ... Sharon let me ask you a question. You ever seen the stuff?"
SHARON. "God, Dawn. I've seen it. But it doesn't taste like this. *(They break into giggles.)* Hey, Dawn, you want another refill?"
DAWN. "Sure, honey, fill it up." *(Sharon takes the mug and Exits from the room.)* Ohh, she was letting go. After she goes to get the stuff, I scope her place. Guess what, she's got tons of books. Big surprise. In front of her books she's got pictures. She got a couple of her with this tall blonde dude. Must be the boyfriend she's not sure about. I can see why, dude's got a sneaky kind of smile on his face. She's got pictures of family too. One of a guy who's probably her brother. He looks cool. And there's her parents who never stand close to the guy or Sharon. She's a cute little girl. I like the picture of her in an Easter hat with white gloves, sticking her pocketbook out. She's sweet but her mother still stands away from her.

(SHARON Enters with DAWN'S present, giggles.)

DAWN. "Sharon, I think I'll wait on this. Open it on the 25th. If that's okay with you?"

SHARON. "Yeah, Dawn, sure." I've got to hold it together. I'm already debating about the toys in the closet. I'm wondering if Dawn's going to think I'm crazy for having them all. I mean I'm twenty... I'm thirty-two-years old. What am I doing with them? Maybe I should just bring out five? "Dawn, I've got something for you, but you've got to turn your back. Shut your eyes."

DAWN. "Okay, girl, but this better be good." *(SHARON Enters with five stuffed animals wrapped in plastic.)*

SHARON. "Okay you can turn around now. Open your eyes. I don't want to be pushy or anything. But since it's Christmas, I thought the kids might like these..."

DAWN. "Hey, fuck the kids. What about me? You got anymore in there?"

SHARON. *(SHARON Exits. From offstage:)* "Got a whole department store in there. Check it out." *(From offstage stuffed animals wrapped in plastic come flying onstage.)*

DAWN. "Teddy Bears, Betty Boops, little lambs, dolls with wedding dresses..."

SHARON. *(SHARON reenters.)* "Sorry I don't have German Shepherds or unidentifiable canines. But you can take all of them.

DAWN. "All of them?"

SHARON. "Yeah, Merry Christmas." *(They cross to DAWN'S area loaded with stuffed animals.)* I help Dawn take the stuff home. I needed the air anyway. We went stumbling up the street singing Christmas carols, we looked like a portable drunken Toys-R-Us. Dawn didn't even mind people scoping us.

DAWN. *(to the tune of "Deck the Halls")* Luckily when we got home the kids were out so I didn't have to hear no shit. I might give them each one toy, but I haven't made up my mind.

SHARON. I helped Dawn set them up on the mantle above the sealed-up fireplace. She was so exact about the placement, it took an hour. *(SHARON and DAWN collapse on couch.)*

DAWN. "Oh don't they look pretty up there. I can just lie here and stare up at them. Make up little stories. Who's doing what to who — I'll kill the kid who lays a hand on them... Hey, Sharon. Let me ask you something ... How much did all this shit run you?"

SHARON. "I didn't buy these. They were presents. From a long line of previous boyfriends."

DAWN. "You must go out with some weird dudes. Giving you stuffed animals?"

SHARON. "I like stuffed animals."

DAWN. "Hey that's cool. I like them too. Didn't have any as a kid."

SHARON. "Well, neither did I. I guess that's why I held on to them for so long ... My mother wouldn't allow them. My father would bring me home little presents. Teddy bears mostly. And I could play with them for a couple of days. Then my mother would make me box them up to take to the Salvation Army. Said other people needed them more than me and that I was too old for them."

DAWN. "Stop! How old were you?"

Sharon. "Eight."

Dawn. "Eight? That's fucked up."

Sharon. "Yeah."

Dawn. "Hey, Sharon, maybe we'll take the kids over to Rockefeller Center. I'll bundle them little fuckers up and we'll go see the tree all lit up. That's something I always wanted to do. What do you say? Sharon, what's the matter, you don't like Rockefeller Center? ... Oh, you want your stuff back. You're missing them already?"

Sharon. "No, I don't want the dolls back. Really, they're yours. It's just that I'm going to California for a few weeks. I wish I was going to be here with you for Christmas."

Dawn. "Hey, it's cool. I get over. Always do. You going to be with family out there? Kick your Momma's ass?"

Sharon. "God no! My boyfriend is taking me."

Dawn. "Hey, this dude got a name?"

Sharon. "Ahh yeah ... it's Norbert."

Dawn. "Shit. Norbert! Girl, you got to cut him loose."

Sharon. "We're going to give it one more try again."

Dawn. "Hey, nothing to be ashamed of. You need your strokes, too."

Sharon. "Yeah well, we'll see about that. I'm taking a book just in case. Hey, maybe we can squeeze a trip in to the tree tomorrow or the next day?"

Dawn. "Hey, Sharon, you got your own shit to get ready for the trip. I'll see you when you get back."

Sharon. "Okay. It's late. I better get going."

Dawn. "Dust off the back of that dress. You got dog hair all hanging off your butt. Don't forget to send me a postcard and have a Merry Christmas. I mean that girlfriend."

(LIGHTS change. SHARON crosses downstage right. DAWN remains on couch. FRANKIE plays the Casio, "Jingle Bells.")

SHARON. I wasn't having a very Merry Christmas in California. I mean, eating sushi in Marin County on December 25th is not exactly my idea of a good time. So I gave myself a little present, I dumped my asshole boyfriend for good. God I love change. I spent the rest of the time in San Francisco. I could actually consider living there. It's about seven years behind New York City in terms of decay. I sent Dawn a postcard. Timed it just right so if the post office didn't fuck it up, it would make it to her house on Christmas Eve. I chose one of the Golden Gate Bridge, kind of a foggy one. I wanted her to know I was thinking of her.

DAWN. *(Rises, stands downstage left.)* I was expecting my lease from the landlord in the mail, but Ebenezer Fucking Scrooge didn't send it. I did get a postcard from Sharon of some foggy-ass bridge. Said she was, "Stroke, stroke, stroking all the time." Adds that she misses me and whatnot ... Looking for something special to bring me back. Girl, bring me back a pan of gold. Anyway she signs it,

SHARON. "Love, Sharon."

DAWN. Not L-U-V. Love. You know what I mean...

(LIGHTS and music fade, DAWN and SHARON Exit. FRANKIE steps into the light.)

FRANKIE. Christmas sucked. Just like I knew it would. I didn't fuck up. I got everything on my list. Worked hard to get it, too. It wasn't me, it was James. See, he had to be running his mouth as the kids opened their presents. He took Tawny's Cabbage Patch Preemie and practicly checked up its butt. Says, "Where did you get all these things?" I tell him I been washing windshields and I've been working as a messenger on the sly. He adds his mouth in, "Hey boy, you may be working on the sly, but you ain't been delivering no envelopes." I just ignore his shit. Watched my Moms face as she opened her gift. I got her a VCR and a little pearl necklace. She starts crying she's so happy. James can't stand it. Says, "Hey, baby, if I was selling my tail, like your son here, I'd get you that shit and more." Oh, I went off. Tried to kick that mother fucker's ass. He took my De-luxe Casio and smashed it right in half. If I had a knife on me, I would have killed that nigger. He's one jealous mother fucker. Knows I'm better than him. Cause I got an enterprising spirit. But I didn't have the powers that night, so he beat me. My Moms gets crazy with tears. So I went up on the roof. *(He races up to the roof.)* Had something on my mind. Call out to the X-Men. All the brothers show up. Tell me a few secrets and show me a power I can't use till the right time. Made me promise.

(DAWN and FRANKIE share the LIGHT.)

DAWN. I could hear him up there stomping around, I thought the plaster would fall from the ceiling again. James tries to hold me back, but I ran up to that roof. "Frankie." I saw him standing on the ledge. I was afraid to move. I thought I might scare him. Send him over. So I just stood there. Watching him. He was talking to someone who wasn't there. A name I didn't recognize. After a few minutes he came down off the ledge. I tell him, "Frankie, baby, you're my blood ... there's nothing that comes between us. Not James, not no one. Frankie?" He didn't hear me. That kid was so far gone he just walked right past me. And it wasn't drugs. He had this other look on his face. Kind of a trance. I went out to the street, called Janet asked her "What the hell am I going to do with that child? He could have gone over. Sweet Jesus he could have fell..." She tells me to come in tomorrow and we'll discuss "options." She thinks he's probably safe for the night. Yeah, right. I hang up that phone, go upstairs and just stare at Sharon's postcard of that foggy-ass bridge and listen to Frankie breathing in the next room.

(LIGHTS fade on FRANKIE and DAWN. Up on SHARON.)

SHARON. When I arrived in Newark my baggage was late so I figured I'd pick up my messages. There was a message from Janet saying "urgent." So I called. While I was away, Frankie tried to kill himself. Jesus Christ. I hung up the phone and sat down by the baggage carousels and just watched my two bags going round and round, never being able to catch up with each other. I almost started crying but the security guard was giving me weird looks, so I left. I thought about going straight to Dawn's but it was so late I just went home. The next morning when I got to work Frankie was standing in the lobby. I brought him into my office. "Frankie I'm real glad to see you. How are you doing?"

(FRANKIE appears at SHARON'S office.)

FRANKIE. "I'm cool. Don't I look different? See, while you were gone I went through the change. I'm okay now. I got the powers."
SHARON. "I see. Is that what you came to tell me?"
FRANKIE. "Ah yeah. And I want you to do something for me."
SHARON. "Sure Frankie what is it?"
FRANKIE. "I'm leaving just as soon as I get some travel plans together..."
SHARON. "Where are you going?" *(FRANKIE stares at SHARON. Looks up as if hearing a voice.)*
FRANKIE. "Sorry. Since you're not part of the family I can't disclose the location."
SHARON. "Have you told your Mom where you're going?"
FRANKIE. "No. See things ain't too cool with my Moms at this present time. So what I want you to do is to take care of her after I split. She's gonna need help with the kids and whatnot. And I've saved some money to help with the bills so you take it..." *(Takes out a wad of money.)*
SHARON. "Frankie I really think you need to sit down with your Mom and tell her what's going on with you. She cares about you very much and she'll be devastated if you just leave."
FRANKIE. "Yeah well that's why I want you around to help her. Now you'll do this for me, right? *(He jams the*

money into SHARON's hands.) You're not pissed at me for never showing up to learn the computer? You wouldn't hold that against me?"

SHARON. "God, no."

FRANKIE. "Cause I really did want too get over here. But something always happened. Fucked with, excuse me, messed with my plans."

SHARON. "I know how that is. But Frankie I've got an idea, if you could just postpone your trip for a few weeks you could start working here. Learn all about the computers maybe even make some money. We could talk to Janet and your Mom and try to find some other living arrangement..."

FRANKIE. "Yeah I might be able to do that. Do you still have my tape?"

SHARON. "Of course. You want to see it now?"

FRANKIE. "Yeah."

SHARON. "Okay, I'll be right back."

(SHARON Exits. Lights change. FRANKIE is suddenly covered in an eerie green light. A computer like musical tone begins to be heard and grows in volume under FRANKIE's monologue.)

FRANKIE. "Check it out. It's just like THE DOOMSMITH SCENERIO in the Classic X-Men. "It begins with an ending and perhaps the breaking of a man's heart..." My heart. The heart of Frankie X-Avier ... A mutant. A full brother of Wolverine. Nightcrawler. Colousus. Dazzler. He'll be demonstrating his full powers at a special showdown. Watch for him." *(FRANKIE disappears. SHARON Enters holding the tape.)*

SHARON. "Frankie? Frankie?" When I came back with the tape he had disappeared.

(SHARON Exits. LIGHTS up on DAWN.)

DAWN. I was up almost all night waiting for Frankie to come home. When he finally showed up he tells me he went over to the Bronx Botanical Gardens and fell asleep looking at the stars. Said he woke up, locked in. What could I say? I feel like I'm walking on eggshells around that child and it's getting to me. I can't eat, I can't sleep, all I do is worry about him. I've been seeing Janet almost every other day since it happened. She tries to get me to go over my feelings, discuss options, the whole deal. I don't want to talk about my own self, I want to help Frankie. Anyway the next morning I go in for my appointment with Janet, my head is so full of problems I forgot that Sharon was back until Janet handed me the phone in the middle of my therapy session. She's extra cheery so I know she's already been on the walkie-talkie with Janet, got the full report. I tell her "Hey, I can't hang on this phone very long. So let's get together. This afternoon. It's my birthday. Capricorn. So bring a present. Hey, good to have you back Sharon. I mean that."
(Women meet with two chairs and sit down.)

SHARON. We were supposed to meet at Rockerfeller Center. The spot where the Christmas Tree was. She was forty-five minutes late on the coldest day of the year.

DAWN. "Fucking kids held me up. See, Tabatha took all the dolls off the mantle while I was taking a shower and the dogs ripped them up. There was stuffing all over the place. Betty Boop was the only one that made it out alive. This is what I try to tell you. I get something and these kids fuck it up. It's the story of my life. I should have killed them all by their third birthdays ... Hey just kidding."

SHARON. She wouldn't let me get a word in edgewise.

DAWN. I knew she wanted to talk to me about Frankie. But I didn't want to hear it. It's my birthday. I wanted one day off. "Hey, let's get some strawberry shortcake a la mode for dessert. But don't tell the waiters it's my birthday. I don't want a bunch of faggots singing over me."

SHARON. I discreetly cancel the birthday cake with the candles.

DAWN. "Hey I got a surprise for you..."

SHARON. "Yeah? What is it?"

DAWN. "You're going to be an aunt! I'm pregnant!"

SHARON. "PREGNANT!" Holy Shit! "WAITER!!"

DAWN. "Sharon I know in that training they push y'all to get us to take the pill, but this is a blessing, not a curse. Come on, be happy for me."

SHARON. "Be happy for you? Christ Dawn how can I be happy for you? A lot has happened since I went away. I think we should talk about Frankie..."

DAWN. "Hey Sharon, I don't want to hear it, okay? I am working that out with Janet. Now this is how we got into the shit the last time. You're trying to throw your weight around where it's none of your business.

SHARON. "None of my business! I went to court for you. I stood up for you. I put my ass on the line for you..."

DAWN. "I know you did. Cause me and you are friends, right?"

SHARON. "Right."

DAWN. "We go to the movies, we read books. You know I read that book 'The Color Purple.' Now let's discuss the book ... that 'Dear God' shit..."

SHARON. "Dawn, stop it, I don't want to discuss the book. I want to discuss Frankie."

DAWN. "Well you need to chill on that."

SHARON. "Dawn, I'm not chilling!! We've got to talk..."

DAWN. "Hey Sharon. Come on. You got those German tourists staring over here..."

SHARON. "FUCK THOSE PEOPLE!"

DAWN. "Hey calm the fuck down. What happened to you out there in California?"

SHARON. "Dawn, Frankie came over to my office this..."

DAWN. "When?"   SHARON. "He's in bad shape..."

DAWN. "I'm handling it with Janet. We're trying to find a way to help Frankie. She's trying to hook me up with this place where he can talk about his feelings after school and maybe we can get him into a gifted program or something. Hook him up with computers. Now that's where you come in..."

SHARON. "I don't want to 'Come In.' "

DAWN. "Oh you don't? I thought that's why you signed up with me in the first place. Put yourself all up in my mess. Next thing I know you'll want to be his mother. You're a sneaky girl. I gotta watch you."

SHARON. "Frankie's talking about leaving, traveling

somewhere. He asked me to take care of you and the kids and he left all this money." *(DAWN shudders.)* "Dawn you know and I know this after school program is not enough. He's beyond all that. We've got to do something."

DAWN. "We? We?"

SHARON. "No, listen to me. It's this city, it's just too much. If he could just get out of here for a little while, out of this environment..."

DAWN. "You want to move my son outta my house?"

SHARON. "Just try to calm down and hear what I'm trying to say to you."

DAWN. "I hear you. You want me to give up my son. Turn him over to who? Who do you have lined up to fix him? 'WE'VE got to do something to save him?' You ain't doing shit. 'Cept telling me I'm hurting my child."

SHARON. "Dawn stop it. That's not true."

DAWN. "I trusted you. I thought you was my friend. But now I see you was just bullshitting me along. I see what's going on with my son. He's hurting bad. I'm keeping him real close to me. Cause if I send him out there now, by himself, he'll bug out. No one knows my child like I do." *(DAWN Exits.)*

SHARON. She didn't take her birthday present. It was a necklace with two gold charms. One said Number One Friend. The other said Number One Mom. Shit. What the hell did I expect from Dawn anyway? What did I expect from myself? Who did I think I was? Mother Theresa? Cause it seems to me you have to bea fucking saint in this life to believe that we are not all powerless. Well, fuck it. I ordered a scotch and just sat there and watched the Rockefeller skaters fall on their asses.

(LIGHTS fade on SHARON, up on DAWN.)

DAWN. I'm finished with that girl. I don't need her shit. Tries to come crawling back. Shows up at my house, screaming up to my window. I'm not throwing my keys downstairs. I don't want that girl up here. She's got the nerve to leave the present on the stoop. Fuck her. I'm going to pawn it. Going to start a little fund for the new baby. Get an Aprica stroller. Snuggli, whatnot. Nobody's real excited about this baby, except me. The kids got attitude. James is the worst. I tell him we miscalculated my monthly — I'm pregnant — he split. Stayed out all weekend. Then he comes home on Sunday night and starts in on me. I tell him "Hey, I'm ain't killing no kid. No way. Kids are life. I'm keeping it." I'm just about to go to sleep and I hear something on the roof. My ears are like radar. Frankie! He's standing on the edge. *(FRANKIE becomes visible on the roof.)*

FRANKIE. "My brothers tell me tonight's the night I can use my full powers. Join them on their mission."

DAWN. Oh God, he's up there just like the last time. Same place. But he looks different. He's scaring me. This ain't my son. I'm moving over there slow cause there's something wrong here. Dear God, you got to give me some time...

FRANKIE. "Ha! I can tell by the way she's scoping me that I got the full powers now. Stand back, I don't need you. I'm really an X-Man! I'M A MUTANT. FRANKIE X-AVIER'S A FULL BROTHER. I CAN MAKE MYSELF

DISAPPEAR. I CAN MAKE MYSELF FLY. HEY, CHECK IT OUT."

(As FRANKIE begins to leap, the LIGHTS go to black.)

DAWN. "FRANKIE!!!"

(A few seconds later, the LIGHTS fade up on SHARON.)

SHARON. Janet called and told me that I shouldn't feel responsible. Right. They never covered suicides in the training. She said that Dawn didn't want any help with the arrangements. Well how the hell is she going to get the money to bury Frankie? Is there some sort of fund or do-it-yourself class to show welfare mothers how to bury their dead? Or is she just supposed to wait for the body to disintegrate in the street? Then collect the ashes and scatter them along Times Square? Jesus Christ! I slammed down the phone and went over there ... Dawn was sitting on the fire escape just staring into the distance. Her face looked so incredibly sad. I watched her for a long time, not knowing what to do, what to say. Then she began to go inside, so I called out to her. She turned toward me and suddenly there was no more space between us. I joined her on the fire escape. We didn't talk. We didn't cry. We just stared up at that dirty sky searching for the path he had used to go home. Frankie.

(LIGHTS fade out on SHARON.

LIGHTS up on DAWN.)

DAWN. Frankie kept appearing to me. Just kept showing up everytime I closed my eyes. I asked him things. Did I do something wrong — did I do something wrong? But he wouldn't tell me why he did it. "See, Frankie, I've been through all you've been through, baby, and even somemore. But, hey, I hung in there. You see, that's what it's all about. Holding on to something. Holding on." After a few days he didn't even show up in my dreams. They didn't hold me responsible for him falling off the roof. Just made a report and left me alone. As long as I promised to go see Janet twice a week. That was no big problem. Anyway I had to hang in the apartment cause the doctor told me to take it easy or I'd lose the baby. I told him to chill, that this was my good luck baby. It's hanging in there. When it was time I had to go out to Manhattan Avenue by myself in the middle of the night to get a cab to Bellevue. That was nothing new. The cab driver was nice. Even though he was a A-rab. He was nervous about having a pregnant lady in his car. Their wives don't even undress in front of doctors. But he took me. Didn't even collect the fare. Said it was the baby's first present. I went into labor as soon as I hit the hospital. See, I time it just right now, so I don't have to hang around too long waiting. It was pretty simple, my little girl came out two hours later. 7 lbs. 3 oz. God, I was so happy. I felt like calling somebody...

(LIGHTS cross fade to SHARON.)

SHARON. Months had passed since I had seen Dawn. I neded the time. Anyway. I decided to stop reading that

Merton book. I was getting to the part where he goes to that conference with all the Buddhists. Drops the fan in the bathtub and dies. What conclusion was I supposed to draw from that event? A Saint is the Act of Being a Klutz? Regardless. I didn't want to get to the end. You know how that happens sometimes, even though you know how something is going to end, you keep wishing you could change it? Anyway, in the middle of the night I get this phone call...

(LIGHTS find both women on the phone.)

DAWN. "Hi It's Dawn. You know Dawn."
SHARON. "Dawn"...
DAWN. "Hey, guess what? I'm over at Bellevue. I didn't bug out. Just wanted to let you know that I had my good luck baby. IT'S A GIRL! 7 lbs. 3 oz. I'm going to name her after that Diahann Carroll character on 'Dynasty.' Remember Dominique Devereux?"
SHARON. "I only saw the show once."
DAWN. "Well Dominique is one tough bitch. She's always going up against old Alexis, the Joan Collin's character..."
SHARON. "I know who Alexis is."
DAWN. "I figure you need a kick-ass name to deal with this fucked-up world. So I'm starting this child off right. Give her all the ammunition. Dominique is her first name. Sharone is her middle name."

(LIGHTS out on DAWN.)

SHARON. Dominique Sharone ... I didn't know what to say. I tried to get back to sleep but I couldn't. So I snuck over to Bellevue, I bribed the security guard to let me in. Dawn was sleeping so soundly with such a serene smile on her face I couldn't wake her up. So I just tied the fifteen helium balloons to her bed and I went into the nursery and stared at little Dominique Sharone. She's a beautiful child. But she's got lungs just like her mother. She kept wailing, so I said "Hey, chill. You got yourself a good mother. And if you play your cards right, a godmother for life." Then I tiptoed out the door.

(LIGHTS fade on SHARON and up on DAWN.)

DAWN. A few weeks after I got home from the hospital, I got myself a job working part time in a deli. With guess who? ... The Arabs! They're cool. Let me take the baby to work. And it's off book. Seems like so far Dominique is my good luck baby. In the mailbox today there was a card from Sharon. Postmarked from some whack state like Arizona. Said she was down there for a week or two visiting with her mother trying to work shit out. Do it girl, 'cause that's crucial. Anyway, she sent the baby a hundred dollars! Oh yeah, and this little tiny book. And she wrote a real nice message on the card about a baby bringing all the joy you ever need in the world. And she signed it love, Aunt Sharon. You know, sometimes I miss the girl. And I miss.... But hey, it's cool. I get over. Always do.

(LIGHTS fade to black.)

THE END

GLOSSARY

X-MEN: Popular comic series.
Uzi: High-powered machine gun.
Whack: Crazy.
Evelyn Wood: Speed-reading course.
Legal Aid: Legal services for low income families.
Coliseum Books: A huge bookstore on 57th Street, New York City.
The Great Big B'Wana: "Great White Lord Over the Jungle."
Thomas Merton: 20th century Catholic monk and philosopher.
The Doomsmith Scenario: An issue of "X-MEN."
Mother Theresa: Nobel Peace Prize-winning humanitarian.
Word: Right on.
Chill: Relax.
Winnie Mandela: Black South African human-rights activist/freedom-fighter and wife of jailed African National Congress leader Nelson Mandela.
SPY Magazine: New York City based satire magazine.
F.A.O. Schwartz: Expensive, top-of-the-line toy store.
Sans: Without.
THE COLOR PURPLE: A novel by Alice Walker which was made into a film by Steven Spielberg and stars Whoopie Goldberg as Celie.
Jacoby and Meyers: Lawfirm advertised on TV.

COSTUME PLOT

FRANKIE:
    Red "Wolverine" T-shirt
    Blue acid-wash jeans
    Black, blue and red troop jacket
    Black leather bicycle gloves
    Black leather belt
    White tube socks
    Black hi-top Adidas sneakers
    Black aviator sunglasses
    Bangle earring

  After Intermission:
    Add black sweatshirt with painted claw
    Black acid-wash jeans
    Fly harness

SHARON:
    Electric blue and black houndstooth-check wool jacket
    White linen blouse
    Electric blue silk crop-pants
    Artsy pin
    Watch
    Large silver earrings
    Black leather loafers

  Christmas Scene:
    Add glitzy Christmas wreath pin

DAWN:
>Bright yellow sweatshirt
>Red tank top
>Black print stretch pants
>Purple socks
>Red sneakers
>Black plastic bracelets
>Large gold earrings
>Blue pigtail holder
>Several rings

PROPS

ITEM	WHO	NOTES
Old couch	Set	Dawn's apartment
Two black ladder-back chairs	Set	Restaurant
Phones (2)	Set	Pay phone (Dawn)
		Cordless phone (Sharon)
Wicker chair	Set	Sharon's apartment
Red roses	Sharon	Bouquet
Red/green carnations	Dawn	Bouquet
Computer print out	Frankie	Color Wolverine mock-up
Computer remote control	Sharon	
Con Ed bill	Dawn	
X-MEN Comics	Frankie	
SK-100 Casio keyboard	Frankie	With shoulder strap
Stuffed animals	Sharon	12 wrapped in plastic
Zippo lighter	Dawn	
Paper money	Frankie	
Wrapped Xmas present	Sharon	
Two egg nog mugs	Sharon	
Christmas tree	Set	Decorated w/lights
Two paper coffee cups	Dawn/Sharon	
Computer tape	Sharon	

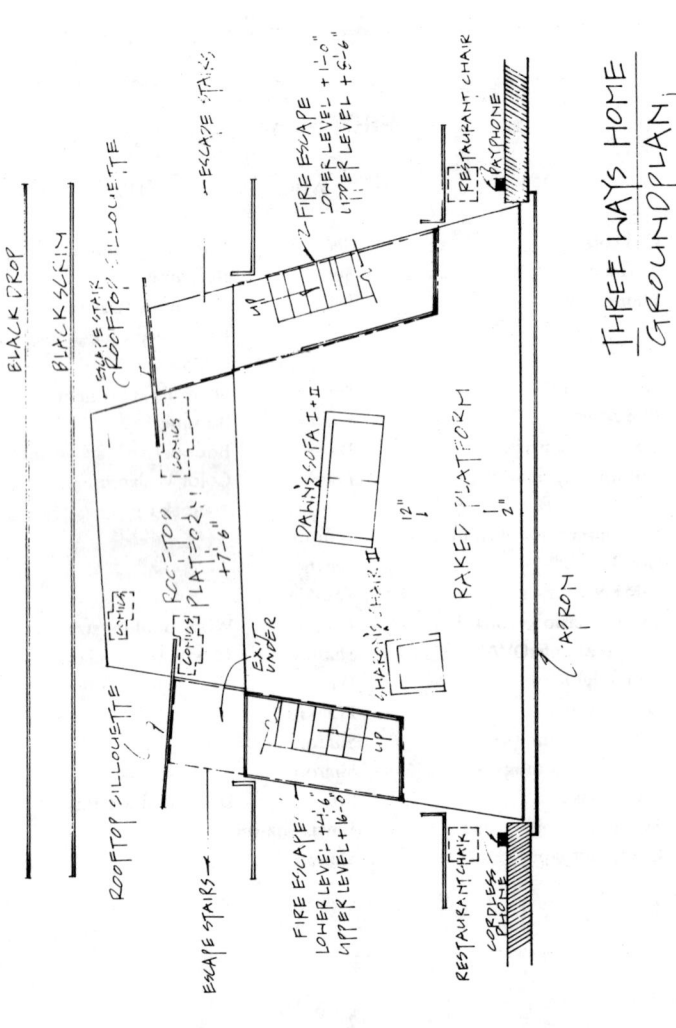

Other Publications for Your Interest

ZOOMAN AND THE SIGN
(BLACK GROUPS—DRAMA)
By CHARLES FULLER
6 men, 3 women—Complex interior/exterior

"As shocking and commonplace as today's and tomorrow's murder headlines . . . an arresting and compassionate piece of work."—N.Y. Daily News. Zooman is scary. He is a teenaged Philadelphia Black youth who senselessly terrorizes Blacks and Whites alike. His most recent crime is the killing of a 12 year-old Black girl on a street filled with people —all of whom are afraid to identify him. The girl's father puts up a sign accusing the community of cowardice for not identifying his daughter's killer; but his friends still won't step forward. Instead, they accuse Zooman of giving the Black community a "bad name" and threaten him with violence of their own. There is an eventual showdown—and then another sign; this time the author's, pointing out the futility of all the preceding violence. Produced in New York to great acclaim by the famed Negro Ensemble Co. ". . . rich in contradiction, in a challenging overlap of right and wrong . . . I found it more absorbing and more satisfying than most of the other serious work I've attended this year."—N.Y. Times. (#28011)

(Royalty, $50-$35.)

EYES OF THE AMERICAN
(ADVANCED BLACK GROUPS—DRAMA)
By SAMM-ART WILLIAMS
2 men, 1 woman—Unit set

What could be more timely than a play about revolution in a small Caribbean island? Something is going on down there, and an American CIA agent posing as a tourist has come to find out exactly what it is. He meets a taxi cab driver who turns out to be the leader of the revolution, who wants to be king—and who eventually will become just that: another tyrant. "Full of riveting scenes and moments."—Village Voice. "Gives some political and moral thought food, and also nourishing roles for three actors . . . It is nice to have a play around willing to raise issues—especially such issues as power, dictatorship and colonialism."—N.Y. Post. (#414)

(Royalty, $50-$40.)

Other Publications for Your Interest

LONG TIME SINCE YESTERDAY
(BLACK GROUPS—DRAMA)
By P.J. GIBSON

8 women—2 Interiors (may be unit set)

Set in suburban Camden, NJ in the early 1980's, this potent new drama by a talented new Black playwright is about a reunion of former college mates, now in their thirties, at the funeral of another friend, who has recently killed herself. These women are prosperous, professional, middle-class Black women who have gone through the turbulence of the sixties and have come out on top in the eighties. These are women you know. At the wake for their sadly deceased friend, the women finally confront the truth about their own lives, and about the suicide which has once again brought them together. All eight roles in the play are well-defined and, needless to say, are quite juicy parts for actresses. This is a literate, humorous, sensitive look at the lives of eight contemporary Black women. It was a SRO success at New York City's New Federal Theatre, which has started so many Black plays and playwrights on the road to recognition. We heartily, fervently recommend *Long Time Since Yesterday*. (#14646)

(Royalty, $50–$25.)

HUNTER
(BLACK GROUPS—DRAMA)
By NUBA-HAROLD STUART

2 men, 2 women (all blacks)—Interior

This moving and, at times, very humorous new drama is about Jerri, a Black mother, and her new boyfriend, Jake. He has spent the night with Jerri at her house. Jerri fixes him a good down-home breakfast—and introduces him to her teen-aged son, Hunter. Naturally, Jake's pretty surprised to hear that Jerri *has* a son. He is even *more* surprised—and filled with consternation—when Hunter comes to breakfast—for Hunter is severely brain-damaged. Jake then has to make a big decision—just how much does he care for Jerri? This touching new play, a *must* for all college, Black and community theatre groups, was a recent success at New York City's famed Actors Studio. The universality of its subject matter makes *Hunter* a sure winner. (#10162)

(Royalty, $50–$35.)